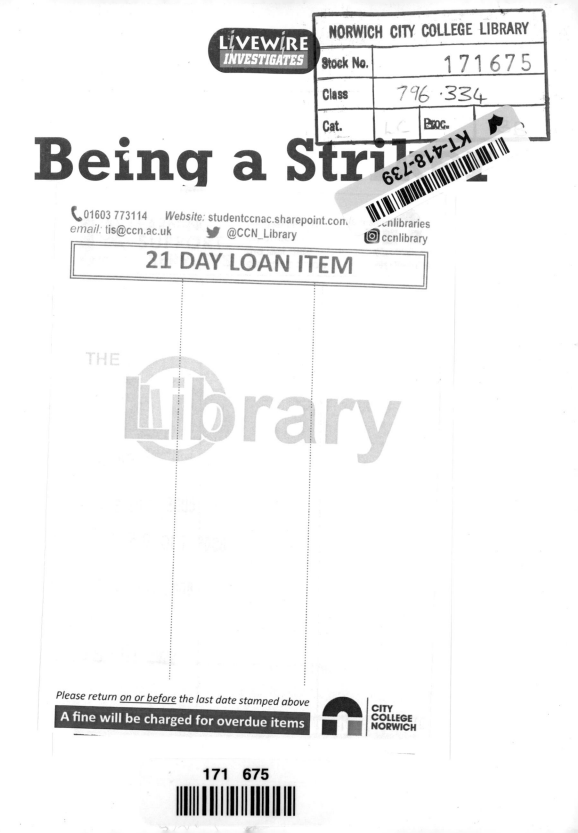

LIVEWIRE
INVESTIGATES

Being a Striker

📞 01603 773114   *Website:* studentccnac.sharepoint.com   ccnlibraries
email: tis@ccn.ac.uk   🐦 @CCN_Library   📷 ccnlibrary

21 DAY LOAN ITEM

THE
Library

Please return <u>on or before</u> the last date stamped above

A fine will be charged for overdue items

CITY COLLEGE NORWICH

Acknowledgements

Cover: Glyn Kirk/Action-Plus.

Photos: © Allsport pp. 5, 10, 15, 17, 20, 22; © Action-Plus pp. 7, 25

Orders: please contact Bookpoint Ltd, 39 Milton Park, Abingdon, Oxon OX14 4TD. Telephone: (44) 01235 400414, Fax: (44) 01235 400454. Lines are open from 9.00–6.00, Monday to Saturday, with a 24 hour message answering service. Email address: orders@bookpoint.co.uk

British Library Cataloguing in Publication Data
A catalogue record for this title is available from The British Library

ISBN 0 340 74722 6

Published by Jamestown Publishers,
a division of NTC/Contemporary Publishing Group, Inc.

First published 1999
Impression number   10 9 8 7 6 5 4 3 2 1
Year   2004 2003 2002 2001 2000 1999

Typeset by Fakenham Photosetting Ltd, Fakenham, Norfolk.
Printed in Great Britain for Hodder & Stoughton Educational, a division of Hodder Headline Plc, 338 Euston Road, London NW1 3BH by Redwood Books, Trowbridge, Wiltshire.

Contents

		Page
1	All the Glory	1
2	Jordan and Jason	3
3	How Do You Keep Fit?	4
4	What is the Main Job of the Striker?	6
5	How Do You Learn to Dribble?	9
6	What is the Secret of Good Forward Passing?	12
7	How Do You Score Headers?	13
8	Tell Us About Shooting	16
9	What If You Have Only the Keeper to Beat?	18
10	Tell Us About Taking Penalties	21
11	Do You Have a Special Celebration When You Score?	23
12	Perhaps One Day ...	26

1   All the Glory

Football is an exciting game.
But the striker's job is the most exciting.
Strikers get all the glory.

Good goals or bad goals.
Easy goals or amazing goals.
It's all the same.
Fans always like a good striker.
As long as they score.

The most famous players are usually strikers.
Just think of some of the brilliant strikers
in the Premiership:

Alan Shearer
Michael Owen
Dennis Bergkamp
Robbie Fowler
Andy Cole
David Ginola
Chris Sutton
John Hartson
Duncan Ferguson
Dion Dublin
Hamilton Ricard.

Think of the last World Cup:

Ronaldo
Suker
Ortega
Henry
Salas
Batistuta
Okocha
Zidane.

Pele was the greatest player of all time.
He was a striker.

2 Jordan and Jason

Jordan and Jason are strikers.
They may not be famous.
But they are pretty good.
They play together
in their local Sunday league.
Their team has just been promoted.
Last season they scored over 80 goals.
Jordan scored over half of them.
Jason makes the goals.
Jordan scores them.

Recently, they were watched by a scout
from a League club.
A scout is someone on the lookout
for good young players.

Jason's favourite player is Juninho.
He is very quick.
Jordan's favourite player is Alan Shearer.
He is very strong.
Both players are brave, strong, fast and fit.
Jason and Jordan try to be as well.

3　How Do You Keep Fit?

Jason　We practise all the time.
And we train one night a week.

Jordan　We go running.
Just four miles.
We like swimming as well.
It all helps to keep us fit.

Jason　We have to watch
what we eat, too.

Jordan　Not too many burgers
and chips.

Jason　Or crisps and chocolate.

Training is important for all players.

4 What is the Main Job of the Striker?

Jordan   Scoring goals!

Jason   It sounds easy.
But it's not.
Strikers can't score goals
on their own.
If I do my job, Jordan can do his.

Jordan   Yes. Jason's job is to get
the ball to me.
My main job is holding the ball up.
Standing with my back to the goal.
Shielding the ball
and waiting for support.
Like Alan Shearer.
You get a lot of bruises.
But that's football.

Alan Shearer.

Jason   Jordan is good
at shielding the ball.
He doesn't let defenders
see the ball.
He is also good
at turning defenders.
Suddenly he is away.
Defenders are left standing
by his speed on the turn.
Watch out Michael Owen!

5 How Do You Learn to Dribble?

Jason Practice.
I used to spend hours
playing football on my own.
Just dribbling up and down
in our back garden.
You need close control.
Like Juninho.
And you need to feint and dummy –
to send the defender the wrong way.
Like McManaman.
You have to be able to change pace.
And direction.
Darren Huckerby is fantastic at that.

Jordan I think you need to be cool too.
It takes cheek to nutmeg
a big defender.
That's when you put the ball
between the defender's legs.

Jason Yes, but defenders always get
their own back with the next tackle.

McManaman in action.

Jordan   But good defenders know
how to close down a dribbler.
The secret is to know
when to release the ball.

Jason   I agree.
Dribbling draws defenders
towards you.
Away from the players they are
supposed to be marking.
Then I try to pass the ball
to one of them.

6   What is the Secret of Good Forward Passing?

Jordan I think it is knowing
where your team mates are
without having to look up.
Paul Merson is brilliant at that.
A good, accurate pass
can split the defence.

Jason Jordan spends a lot of energy
running into space.
It's wasted if we can't
get the ball to him.

Jordan Timing is important as well.
You don't lose your marker for long.
The pass must come straight away.

Jason A late ball puts the striker offside.
A quick pass is the only way
to beat a tight offside trap.

Jordan A good striker takes his
markers with him.
That leaves space for other players.

7 How Do You Score Headers?

Jordan   Easy. Jason gives me
so many good crosses.

Jason   We practise a lot in training.
Crosses and corners.
Inswingers to the far post.
Outswingers to Jordan's head.

Jordan   Jason can cross the ball
while he is running.

Jason   And Jordan knows how
to time his run into the box.
Good strikers can make
a bad cross look good.
Even the best cross
needs someone to head it in.

Jordan   It's something that comes
with practice.
I used to be scared to head the ball.
The trick is to go for it.
I attack the ball.
Call for it.
Make sure it's mine.
Get above the ball.
Meet it with my forehead.
Head it down.

I also practise flicking the ball on.
So other forwards can score.

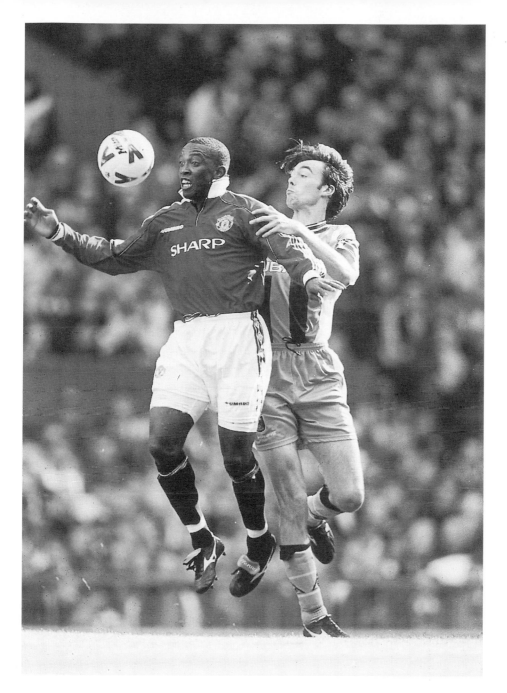

Heading the ball.

8   Tell Us About Shooting

Jason   You must keep your eye on the ball.
Stay over it.
If you lean too far back
you will hit it too high.

Jordan   And shoot low.
That makes it harder
for the keeper to save it.
It is better to shoot wide than high.
You never know,
it might be deflected into the goal.
Put some pace behind your shot.
But accuracy is more important.

Michael Owen shoots low.

9 What If You Have Only the Keeper to Beat?

Jordan
Draw them off their line.
Then you can try to chip it in.
Or take the ball round the keeper.
Then you have an open goal.
Don't let the keeper push you wide.

Jason
It looks easy.
But it's not.
There's no time to think.
If you put your foot on the ball
the defenders will get back.
You have to go for it.

Jordan	If you shoot too soon the keeper has it covered. If you take it too close to the keeper he can grab it with his hands.
Jason	Your team mates think you are going to score. The defenders think you are going to score. The keeper thinks you are going to score.
Jordan	So make sure you do.

A striker always has the keeper to beat.

10   Tell Us About Taking Penalties

Jordan   People think taking penalties is easy.
But everyone expects you to score.
People laugh if you don't.
The keeper has nothing to lose.
And everything to gain.
It's a battle of mind and will.

Decide which side you are going
to put the ball.
Left or right, it doesn't matter.
Then place the ball on the spot.
Don't look at the place
you have chosen to kick the ball.
Stare at the keeper.
Make the keeper feel small.
Make the goal feel big.
Remember, accuracy is more important
than power.

Scoring a goal from the penalty spot.

11 Do You Have a Special Celebration When You Score?

Jordan   We used to do a little dance
by the corner flag.

Jason   Jordan tried doing a cartwheel once.

Jordan   Yeah. But I hurt my back.
I was out injured for three weeks!

Jason   Some players dive in the mud.

Jordan   Some players run to the corner.

Jason   Some players do handstands.

Jordan	Some teams jump on top of the striker when he scores.
Jason	Yes, but it's not much fun when you are at the bottom of the heap.
Jordan	These days, Jason and I just slap hands. We can't show off after every goal. We score so many!

The England team celebrates a goal.

12   Perhaps One Day ...

That scout from the League club
is still watching Jason and Jordan.
They hope he will give them a trial.

Perhaps they will be given a chance.
Perhaps they will become
professional footballers.
If they do, watch out
for Jordan and Jason.
One day they might be famous.
Almost as famous
as Juninho or Alan Shearer.

If you have enjoyed reading this book, you may be interested in other titles in the *Livewire Investigates* series.

Basketball
Being an Actor
Being a Goalie
Being a Model
Being a Striker
Boxing
Bungee Jumping
Climbing the World's Highest Mountains
Hang Gliding
The Last Great Race on Earth
Motocross
Running with the Bulls
Skiing the Impossible
Stunt Flying
Surfing and Snowboarding
White Water Thrills
The World Cup